Published by Out-Spoken Press,
Future Studio,
237 Hackney Road,
London, E2 8NA

A CIP record for this title is available from
the British Library.

First edition published 2019
ISBN: 978-1-9160468-4-9

Artwork:
Ben Lee

Printed & Bound by:
Print Resource

Typeset in: Baskerville

Out-Spoken Press is supported using
public funding by the National Lottery
through Arts Council England.

Epiphaneia

Richard Georges

Acknowledgements

I would like to express my gratitude to the following publications and their editors where these poems first appeared: *The Poetry Review, Reservoir, L'Ephemere, Susumba, PUNCH, Visual Verse,* and *The White Review.*

My undying thanks to Tavia and my family for allowing me my writing life, and gratitude for my litany of supporters and collaborators including: Anthony Anaxagorou, Tony Shearsman, Michelle Tudor, Peter Barnfather, David Knight Jr., Priscilla Hintz Rivera Knight, Joseph Hodge, Patricia Turnbull, Natalio Wheatley, Sauda Smith, Cedric Turnbull, Katherine Smith, Vladimir Lucien, Loretta Collins Klobah, Andre Bagoo, Ishion Hutchinson, Rajiv Mohabir, Raymond Antrobus, Shivanee Ramlochan, Sophia Walker, Sandeep Parmar, Preti Taneja, Pascale Petit, Kaveh Akbar, Lasana Sekou, John Robert Lee, Traci O'Dea, Freeman Rogers, Marsha Pearce, Ayanna Gillian Lloyd, Tanya Batson-Savage, Alscess Lewis-Brown, Will Barrett, Jill Abram, Ann-Margaret Lim, Cadwell Turnbull, Tiphanie Yanique, Emily Berry, Kamaal Lettsome, Arturo Desimone, Des Seebaran, Jannine Horsford, Simone Leid, Ana Portnoy Brimmer, Erika Jeffers, and April Glasgow. Forever appreciation to my teachers and mentors in this poetry thing, in particular Ruth Ellen Kocher, Matthew Francis, Denise deCaires Narain, and Sam Solomon.

Contents

epiphaneia (e-pē-fä'-nä-ä).

An appearing, appearance.
often used by the Greeks of a glorious manifestation
of the gods, and especially of their advent to help; in
2 Macc. of signal deeds and events betokening the
presence and power of God as helper.

for Mona K., for Leslie
for Will, for Esther
for all that we have found
for all that we have lost

Arise, shine, for your light has come

Epiphaneia

How else do we know that we are alive?
Channel a way for yourself through this world;

warm your bones; make life amidst the strife.
What are poems but prayers? An unfurling

of hope, wonder — the words come like a gale
about my head. And then the waves of tributes.

Another gone.
           Now Shabine, make your books our gaol.
See the streaking swift, hollow your canoe.

Out there on the blue, good poet, dance.
I'll stand here, my hand shielding my eyes from

the reddening sun, until the old man's
salted head slips under the horizon.

What am I to do with all that you give,
except to fight, to work, to love, to live?

Dead Reckoning

They say birds always find their way back home
        but home is a nowhere — a memory; a never was.

Do wings remember spaces in the air
        the way we might a place? A field of rice?

How do you fly *back* to that? Away from
        a tomb of fears, this place yearning for you…

Some years ago, I lay bright flowers on
        my grandmother's grave. Years before, I see

my grandfather's ashes taken by the
        furrowing wind in the Bocas islands.

I am not myself nor have I ever been
        something apprehending the sun

and other bright celestial objects
        thinking: *this is a tapestry in orbit*

around me. I am completely convinced that
        we are the last creatures to discover

how to be in the world. My beard grows wild.
        My children brush past me in the darkness.

Their chattering voices fill my ears and
        then my chest and I cannot hold it in.

I am always coming home.

On Remembering, Or Dreams of Remembering

I am forgetting myself. I forget myself
    in the rolling cane, knee high and wondrous,

ecstatic and lost. There was a ravine in Caroni I peered
    into once, it was filled with a gleaming

alligator — its back full of ridges sharp as teeth
    threatening the sky. I forget if these memories

are dreams, (I don't know which I should trust more).
    In a torrent, my father and brother move

a sleeping snake. A tree has fallen in the way,
    my father and brother must move it in the rain.

I enter a room. Turn on a light. A tarantula sits
    on my bed, black hairs bristling in the halogen.

He bids me sit. I sit. He raises two rust-tipped legs
    as if in question — *am I home?*

Too Full of Vermouth and Cigarette Smoke

when I leave I want there to be a carpet of poui
           and the scent of fresh dew and longing

rain sweeping into the harbour and over
           the mountains like walls of grey,

my daughters giggling as they are now,
           I am too full to be remembered like this,

goodbye comes in the languages I cannot remember,
           I cannot understand anymore

how many different ways there are to say *harvest*,
           to feel the coarseness of the seed

on your tongue when the magic of the fruit
           has disappeared with the guinep's flesh,

how you can spit into dirt and grow something
           beautiful. I know I shall be leaving soon, so

let there be seats for the coffee drinkers
           (grounds wet like earth). When I am gone

do not tell anyone I am gone.

Genealogies

Do not tell me a thing does not do what
it does — that these chains (now plated in gold)
are no longer chains, or that from above
the clouds no longer look like drowned bodies
washed ashore in the rolling surf.
                                             I must
go to my mother to learn the real names
of the gorgeous objects in this greened world,
of the beauties that can drive the body
to exhale its life in one purpling sigh,
the body that is a precarious house,
assembled in this world but out of time.

But I can no longer trust my mother's
histories. They are not the taut suspensions
my adolescent mind thought them to be.

The blue-black body breaks at its closures,
twisting in a dancing double helix
dripping blood and amazement.
                              We will be.
Home soon. Bowls filled with brown oxtail and broad
beans. At the food stand, an umber dog floats
through the crowd like a leaf.

The Logic of Perceiving

Your tongue will betray itself. It reminds
you what you have hidden in the spaces
of yourself that you can no longer find,
can no longer expose to naked light.
So you give up the tongue. You cut it out.
But your ears misguide you, unsteady you
for all the unopened words that clamour

about — all that is said and unsaid beguiles.
So you fill your ears with sand and water.
You unbalance yourself, can no longer
stand the maddening beauty of the sky.
Lately, you appear to yourself in dreams —
Shakespearean and full of foreboding —
like fathers (made of ash and smoke) pouring

their sins into saucers for sons to drink.
So you put out your eyes, wrap yellowing
bands about your head where they were before.
In this moment, paradise is a place —
a quiet grove to embower yourself,
to stretch the wretched body like vellum
somewhere under the poui's gentle shower

to submerge in this gorgeous too full life.

Rituals

Come, daughter, we must go now to the hill
where our ancestors strode amongst the tall grass
and worked and worked and worked until

The sun still sets its burning light, it will
still open eyes tomorrow, it will still pass.
Come, father, we must go down the hill

Where your blessed ancestors are still,
buried in this earth, where each stone is cast,
and worked and worked and worked until

This earth can stop spinning, or my eyes fill
with salt, or as long as this day can last.
Come, mother, we must go down the hill

Where the water is, beyond the distant sail,
to hear these voices, the ancestors' final gasp,
who worked and worked and worked until

The sun sank like a hurled stone and still
we are here, we are still here holding fast.
Come, children, we must go now to the hill,
and work and work and work until.

Believer

I believe that belief makes things — makes real
the things which can no longer be abstract —
like the massive black hole at the centre
of our galaxy so much darker
than the cruel absence of matter. Of things.
The centre is nothing.

                       The young Rastaman
in the marketplace knows where we come from.
His proud hair locked in an upward spiral —
a supplication. He knows what is made
when nobody remembers to believe.

Pathfinder

Or you can walk down Main Street, discovering
the graffiti histories of this place —

the leaning bricked facades, hollowed like tombs.
Beneath every inch of this ground is blood

and we know that there is nó other way
to navigate a return to yourself.

You can twist your limbs the way trees do,
fingers gripping the firmament, toes deep

in the earth, always and always searching
the deep amazement this world makes of us

and I fear that all you will discover
are other bodies in the same mad dance.

The roads here were worn by horses and mules,
generations of hooves with the good sense

to meander around trees and ravines
since sometimes the swiftest way to a place

is not straight to it, not geometric.
You will find your way. Everywhere is song.

Crown Shyness

It is a cruel truth that much greatness comes from backs
breaking into a field of fireflies and trees that do not touch
each other for fear of shadows falling on their writhing roots.

My children have played among such roots, full
of serpentine twisting, perfectly placed for a toddler's ankle,
or for something dead to grip on the way up from a grave.

I roamed this rugged land as a boy, the hair on my head knotting
like Lord Shiva's, my limbs growing longer, clambering
up the majesty of a giant guava with the other children.

At the top, we could see the surrounding villages amidst the cane,
the three rolling ranges in dusty haze, the ocean (always the ocean),
and the spreading coast of Venezuela — a greyed line on the horizon.

I remember the splitting bark, multi-coloured and peeling,
until the summit where it was a deep burning red, and we felt
like little rulers, our domain as wide as the expanse before us.

And the grave is not its goal

The Storm is Here and a New World is Awakening

Survivor stories begin to meld together:
the hollow wail of galvanize tearing away

       from the rafters; the house opening like the mouth
       of a cavern; the sky, the sea, the hungry storm.
       All of it pouring in.

             They say he held the door,
still, long after the storm had taken him skyward,
like hope.

       And so the cataclysm comes and all
the warnings will not stop the sky devouring
us. Here, every tree has been made a monument,

       every soul a witness that the next world is not,

is not forever a more joyful one than this.
We are all a little less now. We are only

       ever so far from ruin.

             I dream on still nights.

A flying man,

opening a door   in the sky.

An Inventory for Survival

The next morning the coral lay in piles,
heaped into roadside mounds on the island's
southern coast. It's a stretch the sea beguiles

as it wears away the rock embankment,
but the coral stones still remind the eye
of funeral pyres. An enchantment,

perhaps, from when I skirted the coastal
parts of the Essequibo, the Hindu
cremation plots on the ridge; the coast walled

from the highway, only the scant platforms
afire, the dense smoke rising like snakes
in the air. On Tortola, the smoke forms

sparsely on the banks of the ravines, aches
across the burnt hillsides before settling
somewhere above it all. The thing that breaks

us is all there is sometimes. The bettering
of death teeters on obsession, but then
we each come to our private reckoning,

our own single raptures, the damn air
screaming, and us, making bathtub altars,
speaking the names of our children like prayer.

Still Life of a Ruin
for David Knight Jr.

There is a modest house in Huntum's Ghut,
green and white and two-storied and roofless,

its narrow louvers gone, an aperture
where the patio was, and just clean air

where trophies, books, pictures of the children
should be. Still, amidst the crumbling city

there is hope like green shoots pushing up through
the rubble and mud. And now the singing

birds loop like kites, the sun remains a star,
and we are still here — rocks circled by blue.

My friend says goodnight, the hillsides are dark
and peaceful, fields lined with their naked trees

like matchsticks. But this meagre house, roofless
and gutted, vaunts its one door still hanging,

still welcoming. Unblown and defiant.

A Longer Loneliness

Come then. Along the road there will be lovers,
the drinkers assemble where there are no walls,
no dawns or nights, just a ceaseless twilight. And we

lonely wanderers in search of bodies we know
by the clarities of blue-grey light. This place
will teach you how to make your selves small, narrowed

into thinner spaces, always learning anew
that the fire can consume you, the house you build
(your borders, your monuments) can be broken.

We have never been more alive than today.
Look at the greenness blooming from the stiff trees!
The island thrives. Yellow mornings peel away

the clouds. The ticking sea keeps time on the coast.
And do you see the pelicans measuring
the breakers? They still know that there is life here

and they and us and all of this are made of
the same stardust, made with the same stinging love,
made with the same delicate intemperance.

This road we travel can yet be washed away,
erased. But we are here. Now. There is still light.
The drums are thick — there is so much to be found.

Altricial

Remind me again, the way you carry
your people, your family through the stark

silence of the years. How the village grows,
what brilliance can be found in it,

and how toil can mean something, how burdens
were always meant to be laid down somewhere

cool and grassy. That the unspooling years
must mean something besides the laughing stars.

Again. Tell me how a soul moves through the
body the same way bodies move through space —

unthinking and bravely, like something wild
beating waves in the current. This is not

and has never been an ending thing. Birds
do not know where they will land when they fly,

yet few fall like too-ripe fruit from the sky.
The astonishment of exhaustion, winds

too strong to buffet, of God giving more
than their fragility can hope to bear.

Remind me again, how people become
weights, or how they become feathers. Then wings.

The Year Has Become More Beautiful

There is no power in the walls. The noisy nights rattle on.
So, I fill my cup with as much ice as it can carry
and flood it with as much drink as it will hold.

Green vines cover everything that was ruined.
The rabble rousers light fires on foundations.
They drink, they smoke, they laugh loudly — there is more here than joy.

Every morning I walk past a fallen tree,
its broken boughs wet and flowering purple.
This is a different kind of broken now.

I've begun to learn that *devastated* does not mean *dead*,
that ruin can be resplendent,
that what has been emptied can be filled.

This year has become more beautiful for the scars.
I've heard folk measure pain by hurricane.
You can still look through some windows and see only sky;

still see gaping homes like cupped hands.
The day is full of heat, the screaming behemoths clear the rubble,
your morning walk is barricaded by afternoon. The map shifts.

I know there are no such things as endings or beginnings.
No cycles to measure. No useful predictions. The prophets
are all mealy-mouthed and impotent. There is only this ball,

madly spiralling through space — and that is the most reassuring thing.
From the windows in our bedroom I used to watch our neighbours:
their busy lives, the tempests.

Tonight our view is clear out to the channel,
the moon making the waves sparkle silver.

Thanks
after W.S. Merwin

Is there a light more stunning, more arresting
than the one at dawn? I am talking about
the slow creeping ignition of the sky,
the clouds becoming kaleidoscopes. We
that watch become fiercely devoted to it.

Beauty is an amnesic devotion.
We forget that every part of this land
is a one-time grave, or that we were all once
a part of the heaving mass seeking to land
on a greener patch of earth. But beauty kills.

The watching few will remember the past
while the rest of us will live like flowers,
each petal a parchment that the day inscribes,
its birth a certain light that the night will obscure.
All around us the living are slowly not

living anymore. We wonder when we will
stop surprising ourselves with our own
mortality. How a body can survive
a war, a storm, a marriage unscathed yet
fall into itself over afternoon tea.

All around us this living is dying but
the dying is living too. So let us linger
in doorways with our too long goodbyes,
let us laugh, let us drink our wine, let us
say thanks though no bright soul is listening.

Notes on Road Town

1.

Does light dance the same way in your eyes as mine?
Do not prolong your flight through the eddying air,
Carthage beckons — as always.
                                    There I imagine,
we should have all been poets,
until avulsed by Rome, winged with rubble,
scribbling notes at the base of magnificent columns.
But the daunting day is relentless, my city
looks a wreck beset by weeping clouds, the sea
will not listen to reason, and the punitive clock
does not compromise its metronomic rhythms.

2.

The rains come again to deluge the ghuts,
the island, briefly, returns to a browning in the sea,
the men go down to their boats through the mangrove's
mangled roots.
                        Words bud in the mouth, this is all
a hymn. Look at the children, skittering like birds,
a capon poises himself on an unfinished wall,
even he knows the extent of his dominion,
the acreage of his call, the blueblack of his feather.
The ghut waters thunder in backdrop, the dew
has formed in beads on everything — what remains
of the corrugated roofs, the broken, limping hills.

3.

What is *the beautiful, needful thing*? The fish lie in rows,
bare and blue in the ice. Their bodies, radiant in the tray
of the fisherman's pickup, the sun skipping along their scales,
their eyes like saucers of ink. I cannot discern where
the lure lanced, when the water broke into nothing,
into death's frantic dance. The road rumbles, a crowd
congeals, and the exhausted fisherman,

Guinness in hand, flares a gold-toothed smile
at his congregants.
                              Their voices, ascending,
rebound off each other like breakers.

4.

The fly hums his impromptu arc,
simple sweat and, you know: *what must is must is.*
Gifts must break boredom. And the water
washes up alongside our cars, running,
always running, and we fear it
coming inside, breaking things as it does.
The word [the world] and all its attentions,
the scientists are in terror, and still
the water is rising.
                              The townspeople
concur, we must build our new homes in the air.

5.

Perhaps from a cloud perch, or from a fine
cratered moon, storms can be beautiful things.
Exemplars of asymmetry, of a natural mechanics
[as natural as sound], of how they form a language
their own that both poet and fisherman understand.
        When the unmaking is stilled, the land
a negative space, there are still ghosts outside,
unstilled. There are still so many winds still
to come. That blue porcelain will not remain
long above us so plainly, so unremarkable.

Thank you for all your blessings and your miracles

Still,

We drove past so many stoic villages, the rows of rice fields,
the centuries of molasses still thick in the nose.

At Parika, the boats sit still in the Essequibo's silt (thick as molasses)
tied to obelisk rods, their bright favours like crude flags

and the receded water, how brown but still radiant.
Beloved, we must seize what we can in our arms,

spirit whatever we can carry from the conquerors.
The sweet interlude still runs out into the world

like the cold rushing tide and claims it like a dream.
Do bloody fingers cross these hearts? I still came home.

We said our prayers with tongues swollen with language,
gripping our lies like lines, that our bodies were still not bodies

that every part does not speak its own corrugated talk
that navigates the brutal architecture of light and still sound

with equal parts grace and inelegance. The boys and girls
still must make their way down the remnants of the road.

Listening

What could I have known of the easeful ways
of sliding through this world? A dew drop
descending the petal's sloping splendour;

this same moon that rose over great beasts
and effervescing pools now rises
over your back's prickling flesh and —

there is only so much water within us,
yet we are all pooling through our bodies,
pretending to be solid masses,

to be beings that matter, bodies
with obligations to other bodies.
For instance, death need not be

such a final, final thing. The days
heave along at a lazy pace.
If there were still leaves in this naked place

they would be still too, or at least listening
for the sighing tides of the Atlantic,
for the shuddering clouds' fearsome report,

for the cyclic storms of trauma tracing
the exhausted courses of our ancestors,
for the chanting sky's low hollow sound.

Postlude: This beach is not a beacon

This beach is not a wind-vane,
is not a beacon beckoning your bodies,
is not a measure of resilience;

The sea may be roaring,
the seagrapes may be singing their
praises to the constant wind;

The morning sets the night alight,
the morning begins like a fire
on the dark line of the horizon;

The vines ripple over the bony trees,
their broad leaves dripping light,
their leaves veined with a lively purple;

And the beach, the beach is not a beacon,
a crescent moon of sand and coral,
that pulls the busy sea into itself.

Essentials

What do you need?
As many batteries as you can carry.
Your radio is your altar.

All the water you can buy,
because what falls out of the sky
can only drown you.

Nails. Good ones for concrete.
Ones that will hold to your house
and pray like you do.

-

What do you have left?
Faith, because what else can you take with you?
Grow accustomed to the bleating blades of helicopters.
Forget exactly when the soldiers arrived.
The soldiers were always here.
Damnit. Why are all the poets dying?

-

How will I find you?
Find your bearings in the darkness
by the light in the channel.
The light in the channel is a warship.

-

What do we do when we get there?
Use anything you can to collect the rain.
Cup your hands to your ears if you must.
They must clear the mounds of coral from the roads first.
The coral are not bones.
They are bright flowers.

The Transmutation of Grief

The little boy next door has taken to beating boredom
on a drum kit   he has a mouthful of fireflies

the hollow trees and their spalling barks are monuments
the whole valley echoes for him.

Origin

A rising reef   the bubbling abyss
God parting his hair   the ocean become
milk churning on a majestic turtle
the word   spoken   pull earth from water
did you not question   did you not wonder why
this world always begin and end with ocean?

Becoming an Answer
to Errol Percival aka Daïikiru Maximillion

Peace be unto the wanderer, his stoic quarter
of Paradise between the wave's rigid arc and sand;
or still shifting earth; or crowded dock; or rotting pier. '

How this listing sloop resembles the clock's slipping hand,
a grand rising, a restless stirring beneath his hair.
May his God bless him and all his worthless endeavours

worthy too of course. And if *I become an answer,*
know that the way must be the question.

Heartache is for Lovers,
and Other Lies We Tell Ourselves

And here, the island reclines on its side,
nothing but rippling blue and stippling light.

Nobody here is ever quite here enough —
the tourists adore the unpeopled shores,

and *the locals*, the locals are unsure.
Is there anything of worth that remains

besides this kingdom of fossilized gods?
Someone said that "men only worsen,"

and I believe lies like this, the ones that
pack up our best lives lived, and bury

them in reason.

Thoughts on Reincarnation

If this is it, and we don't reappear
somewhere as polar bears queueing for ice,

then, perhaps, I might admit, that this life
was (is) something. But I'm afraid I fear

being pulled into an unknowing cycle,
challenged again, to get the damn thing right.

There's no way to grow such an appetite.

Prometheus the Titan Descends with Fire

And why do you learn language? That fire that
too quick consumes, burns boughs black.

But the earth and I, formless and frothing
in our newness, can be found with words,

can first be made real by the moving mouth,
or unmade, disassembled, by the same.

The word means we no longer recognize
the spirit, cannot conceive the body,

yet can make gods of men and gods mortal.
In the rolling millennia I have learned

the mouth yearns, it consumes our livers,
our lives, what else this little tyrant

leaves behind, takes inside itself, or makes
it has defiled, broken, and made useless.

The mouth names and maims. Call me Anansi.
Loki. Prometheus. Omnipotence.

Who can afford such a cruelty my love?
To love something, somewhere, or worse — someone.

This is my gift to you all.

A Mixtape for Tortola

On a green island,
The cassette frames two cyclones—
Time spinning away;

The black cassette spins,
And the room swells with static—
The storm's ruthless roar;

Bodiless voices,
The gutted, gaping houses—
The still bleeding wounds;

A helicopter,
Its blades frozen in saltire—
A suspended god;

We are listening,
The cyclones spin, but we hear
Nothing but silence.

Love always shines.

Other titles by Out-Spoken Press:

Stage Invasion: Poetry & the Spoken Word Renaissance
Pete Bearder

The Neighbourhood
Hannah Lowe

Nascent
Vol 1: A BAME Anthology

Ways of Coping
Ollie O'Neill

A Greek Verse for Ophelia & Other Poems
Giovanni Quessep

The Games
Harry Josephine Giles

Songs My Enemy Taught Me
Joelle Taylor

To Sweeten Bitter
Raymond Antrobus

Dogtooth
Fran Lock

How You Might Know Me
Sabrina Mahfouz

Heterogeneous, New & Selected Poems
Anthony Anaxagorou

Titanic
Bridget Minamore

A Silence You Can Carry
Hibaq Osman

Email:
press@outspokenldn.com